BRACHIOSAURUS

by Janet Riehecky
illustrated by Jim Conaway

THE CHILD'S WORLD

MANKATO, MN

Grateful appreciation is expressed to Bret S. Beall,
Curatorial Coordinator for the Department of Geology,
Field Museum of Natural History, Chicago, Illinois,
who reviewed this book to insure its accuracy.

Library of Congress Cataloging in Publication Data

Riehecky, Janet, 1953-
   Brachiosaurus / by Janet Riehecky ; illustrated by James Conaway.
      p. cm. — (Dinosaurs)
   Summary: Describes the physical characteristics and probable
behavior of one of the largest dinosaurs.
   ISBN 0-89565-542-X
   1. Brachiosaurus—Juvenile literature.   [1. Brachiosaurus.
2. Dinosaurs.]   I. Conaway, James, 1944-   ill.   II. Title.
III. Series: Riehecky, Janet, 1953-   Dinosaur books.
QE862.S3R532   1989
567.9'7—dc20   89-22069
                                                   CIP
                                                   AC

BRACHIOSAURUS

Millions of years ago the earth echoed
with the thud of gigantic feet. It was the
sound of dinosaurs on the move.

Most of the dinosaurs were huge crea-
tures.

Nearly all of them were bigger than a
man.

Most of them were bigger than an
elephant.

Many of them were as big as a school
bus . . .

and a few were as big as a house! The biggest dinosaurs were the biggest land animals that have ever lived.

One of the biggest dinosaurs of all was the Brachiosaurus (BRAK-ee-uh-sawr-us). This enormous creature stood as tall as forty-three feet. If it had lived today, it could have looked into a fourth-floor window! It measured seventy-five to eighty-five feet long—which is twice as long as a school bus. And it weighed as much as eighty-five tons—which is more than the weight of twelve elephants. The forearm alone of this creature was about seven feet long and weighed almost five hundred pounds. That one bone was bigger than most people!

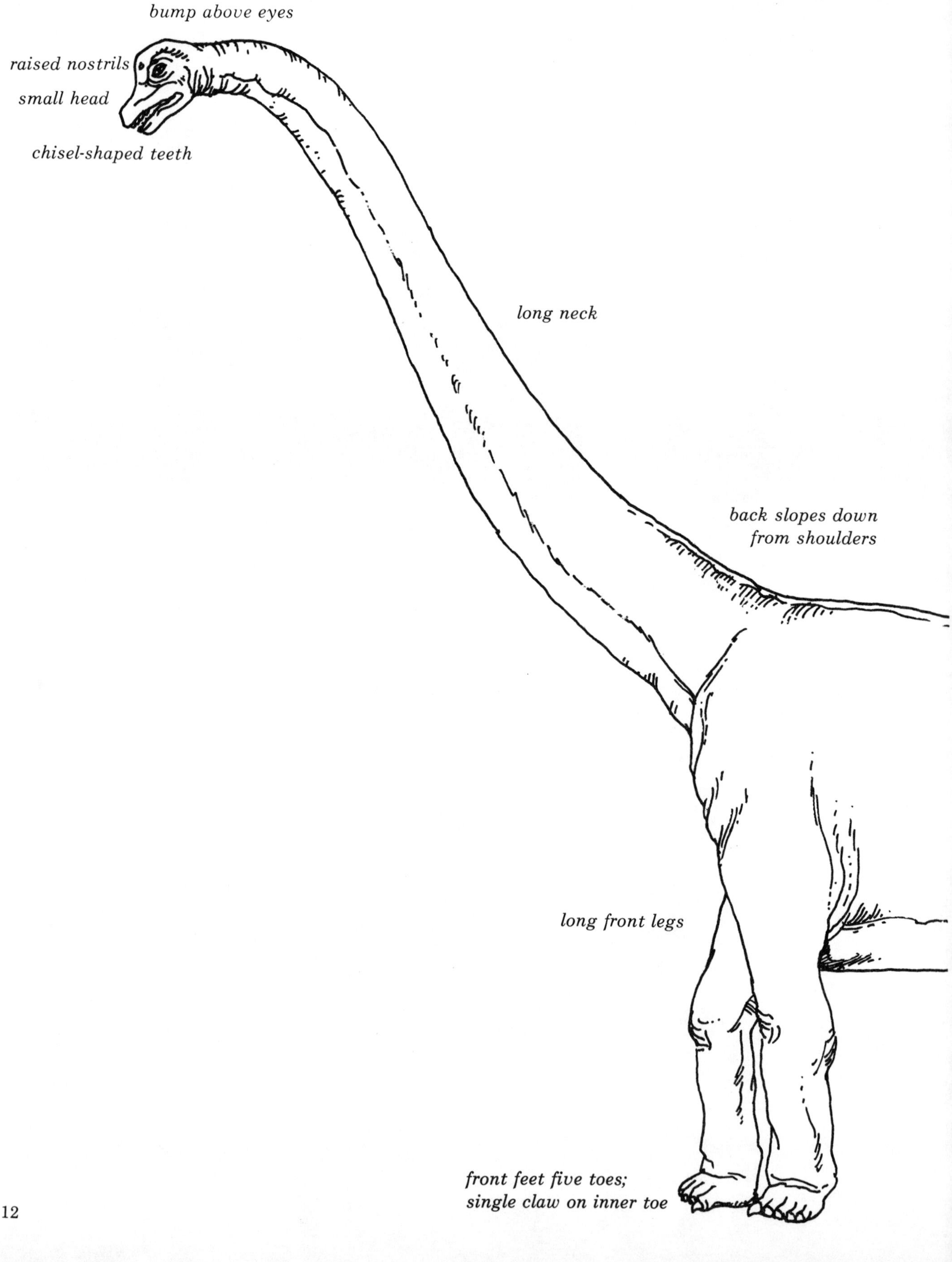

bump above eyes

raised nostrils

small head

chisel-shaped teeth

long neck

back slopes down
from shoulders

long front legs

front feet five toes;
single claw on inner toe

Brachiosaurus means "arm lizard." It was named that because its front legs (or arms) were longer than its back legs. Brachiosaurus and its relatives are the only types of dinosaurs whose front legs were longer than their back legs.

Because of its long front legs, the Brachiosaurus's back sloped down from its shoulders to its tail. It looked something like a fat giraffe with a long tail. On top of its huge shoulders was a very, very long neck. The neck alone could stretch twenty-eight feet—as long as a small flagpole.

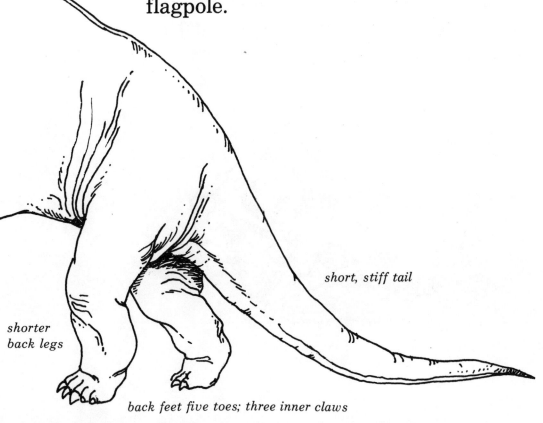

shorter back legs

short, stiff tail

back feet five toes; three inner claws

The head of the Brachiosaurus was quite small for such a large creature. Its jaws were small, but sturdy. They were filled with sharp, chisel-shaped teeth.

Above its eyes, the Brachiosaurus had a large bump. This is where the Brachiosaurus had its nose. This may seem strange to you, but it worked well for the Brachiosaurus. Having its nose up so high meant the Brachiosaurus could swallow and breathe at the same time—so the Brachiosaurus didn't have to stop eating even to breathe!

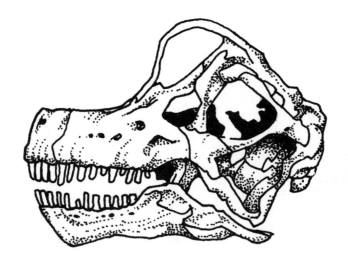

And such a huge creature did need to
eat a lot. Scientists think the Brachiosaurus spent most of its time eating and
eating and eating. It was a plant eater,
and its favorite foods were probably

leaves and pine needles from the very tops of the trees. Some scientists say the reason Brachiosaurus grew so tall was so it could eat leaves that other dinosaurs couldn't reach.

Brachiosaurs probably traveled in herds, eating everything in sight. They moved slowly through the countryside with their tails held out stiffly behind them. If a stream or lake were in the way, the Brachiosaurus would wade through it. But Brachiosaurs probably didn't like the water very much. Their small feet and heavy weight made it too easy for them to get stuck in the mud.

When Brachiosaurs traveled, they covered only about two miles in an hour, but that didn't matter. They went wherever they wanted to go (who would get in their way!), and they weren't in any hurry to get anywhere. As long as there were lots of plants nearby, Brachiosaurs had everything they wanted.

Brachiosaurs didn't even need to run from meat-eating dinosaurs. There were some fierce meat eaters, such as the Allosaurus, alive at the same time. But the Brachiosaurus was more than twice

as big as the biggest one. So if another
dinosaur tried to bother the Brachiosaurus, all the Brachiosaurus had to do
was throw its weight around.

Scientists don't know how Brachiosaurs had their babies. They might had laid eggs, or they might have had their children alive. But scientists do think Brachiosaurs took care of their babies once they had them.

Some scientists think Brachiosaurs set up a "nursery" near where the herd was grazing. Lots of plants and fresh water would have been nearby. In such a nursery, the babies had a safe place to play and to grow. (And they did a lot of growing!) Imagine how the ground would shake as dozens of baby Brachiosaurs jumped and ran and wrestled!

Adult Brachiosaurs would take care of the babies in the nursery. They would protect them from meat-eating dinosaurs, and they probably chewed up leaves and pine needles to make soft food for the babies.

When the babies grew big enough to
take care of themselves, they joined the
herd. The littler Brachiosaurs probably
traveled in the center of the herd, pro-

tected on all sides by the huge adults. You couldn't ask for a better bodyguard than an eighty-five ton Brachiosaurus.

The Brachiosaurus may have been the biggest dinosaur that ever lived, but scientists don't know this for sure. They have found a few bones of three different dinosaurs that may have been bigger.

One of these new dinosaurs has been named Supersaurus. Supersaurus has a shoulder blade that is eight feet long. Its longest neck bone is five feet long. Unfortunately, scientists haven't found enough Supersaurus bones to know much more about the creature. They do think a creature with those bones that large would have been fifty-four feet tall and eighty-two to ninety-eight feet long!

A few years after finding Supersaurus, scientists found Ultrasaurus. Its shoulder blade was nine feet long, and its bones suggested it was as tall as a six-story house! Again there weren't enough bones to be sure what type of dinosaur it was, but this time scientists thought it might be related to the Brachiosaurus.

Scientists thought no dinosaur could be bigger than Ultrasaurus, but just a few years after finding Ultrasaurus, they found more gigantic bones, suggesting an even larger dinosaur. Scientists gave this new dinosaur the nickname "Seismosaurus" — the "earthquake lizard."

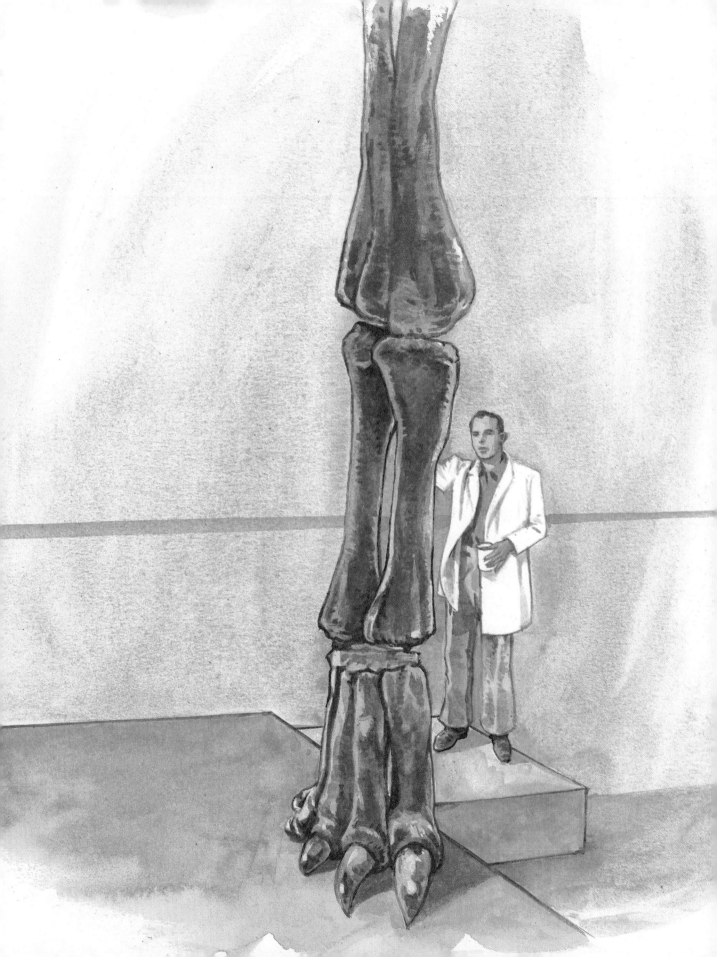

Reptiles grow their entire lives, unlike mammals which stop growing once they become adults. So while it's hard for scientists to say much about the new dinosaurs they've found, they do think their huge size means they lived very long lives —perhaps as long as two hundred years. If a Brachiosaurus lived even longer than that, who knows how big it would get!

Scientists are trying to learn more about these biggest dinosaurs. If they keep exploring, perhaps someday they may discover even bigger dinosaurs—they may find Super-ultra-seismosaurus!

Dinosaur Fun

Scientists are not only interested in what dinosaurs looked like. They also want to know what the dinosaurs' world looked like. For example, what kinds of plants were around for Brachiosaurus to snack on? Scientists find out by studying fossils. Sometimes plants were pressed into mud, leaving a print. After many years, the mud dried out and turned into stone. The prints from the plants are preserved in the stone as fossils.

You can make your own plant "fossil." You will need:
— modeling clay (the kind that hardens)
— a few leaves that you think will make good prints

1. Flatten out the modeling clay.
2. Lay a leaf flat on the clay, with the veins facing down.
3. Press the whole leaf down into the clay.
4. Pick up the leaf. Did it leave a print? Let the clay harden. Repeat these steps with the other leaves.